Under the shadow
of the
Almighty

Copyright © 2021 Rosy Grace Joshua

Hard Cover: 978-0-578-31457-0

Personalized declarations in each page is the author's own rendition of Psalm 91.

Dedicated to all the children of the world

(You say)
I live in the shelter of the Most High and will find rest in the shadow of the Almighty.

(You say)
God alone is my refuge, my place of safety; he is my God, and I trust him.

(You say)
God will rescue me from every trap and protect me from deadly disease.

(You say)
God will cover me with His feathers.
He will shelter me with his wings.
His faithful promises are my armor
and protection.

(You say)
I will not be afraid of the terrors of the night, nor the arrow that flies in the day.

(You say)
I will not dread the disease that stalks in darkness, nor the disaster that strikes at midday.

(You say)
I will not be harmed, though thousands fall all around me.

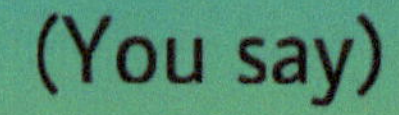

(You say)
I will just open my eyes,
and see how the wicked are punished.

(You say)
I will make the Lord my refuge,
I will make the Most High my shelter.

(You say)
No evil will conquer me; no plague will come near my home.

(You say)
God will order his angels
to protect me wherever I go.

(You say)
Angels will hold me up with their hands so I won't even hurt my foot on a stone.

(You say)
I will trample upon lions and cobras; I will crush fierce lions and serpents under my feet.

(God says)
I rescue you because you love me.
I will protect you because
you trust in my name.

(God says)
When you call
on me,
I will answer;
I will be with
you in trouble.
I will rescue
and honor you.

(God says)
I will reward you with a long life and give you my salvation.

Psalm 91 NLT

1 Those who live in the shelter of the Most High
   will find rest in the shadow of the Almighty.
2 This I declare about the Lord: He alone is my refuge, my place of safety;
   he is my God, and I trust him.
3 For he will rescue you from every trap
   and protect you from deadly disease.
4 He will cover you with his feathers. He will shelter you with his wings.
   His faithful promises are your armor and protection.
5 Do not be afraid of the terrors of the night,
   nor the arrow that flies in the day.
6 Do not dread the disease that stalks in darkness,
   nor the disaster that strikes at midday.
7 Though a thousand fall at your side,
   though ten thousand are dying around you,
   these evils will not touch you.
8 Just open your eyes,
   and see how the wicked are punished.
9 If you make the Lord your refuge,
   if you make the Most High your shelter,
10 no evil will conquer you;
   no plague will come near your home.
11 For he will order his angels
   to protect you wherever you go.
12 They will hold you up with their hands
   so you won't even hurt your foot on a stone.
13 You will trample upon lions and cobras;
   you will crush fierce lions and serpents under your feet!
14 The Lord says, "I will rescue those who love me.
   I will protect those who trust in my name.
15 When they call on me, I will answer;
   I will be with them in trouble. I will rescue and honor them.
16 I will reward them with a long life
   and give them my salvation.

If you would like to receive the gift that God has for you today, say this with your heart and lips out loud.

Dear Lord Jesus, come into my heart. Forgive me of my sin. Wash me and cleanse me. Set me free. Jesus, thank You that You died for me. I believe that You are risen from the dead and that You're coming back again for me. Fill me with the Holy Spirit. Give me a passion for the lost, a hunger for the things of God and a holy boldness to preach the gospel of Jesus Christ. I'm saved; I'm born again, I'm forgiven and I'm on my way to Heaven because I have Jesus in my heart!